LIMONCELLO AND THE GREAT ILLNESS

Written and Illustrated by
Angela Marciano

There once was a little duck named Limoncello.

Limoncello lived in a lazy green meadow with very bright and welcoming wildflowers near a very blue pond.

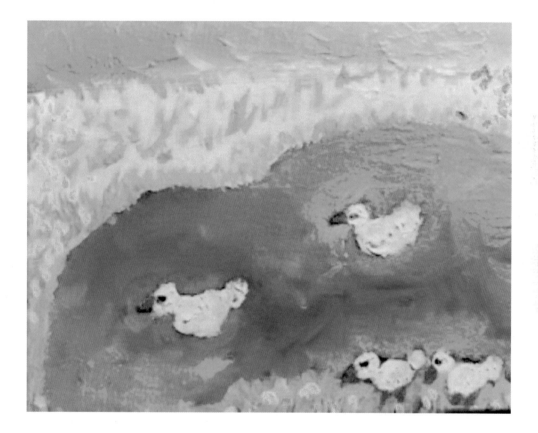

Limoncello was a very busy little duck.
She would swim in her pond with her friends every
day.

She would go to school and learn new things like reading and writing. Limoncello was even learning how to play the guitar.

Limoncello would go on hikes to the pond with her family and would look at the stars in the sky. The stars were very bright and shiny.

Limoncello would play Duck, Duck, Cat in the meadow with her friends. Usually the Cat, Espresso, would win but Limoncello didn't mind that.

She enjoyed playing games with Espresso more than winning the game anyway.

Sometimes Limoncello would just stop what she was doing and smell the poppies that would grow in the meadow. The poppies smelled fresh and clean. Smelling the poppies would make Limoncello joyful.

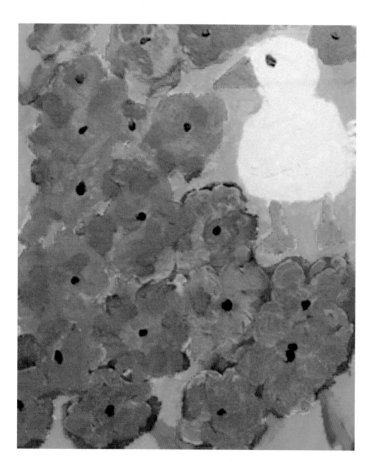

Limoncello was a very happy little duck with very good friends and a family that she loved.

One day there came a great illness over all the land. Doctors talked about the illness and explained how to stay safe and healthy. The Doctors said that little ducks should do seven very important things to protect themselves and others from the illness.

Dr. Andy Mallard

1. Stay Home!

This was easy for Limoncello because she loved her
home and her family.

2. Keep clean. Wash your wings a lot.
Try not to touch your face and beak even when you
have an itch.

3. Leave plenty of space between yourself and others. This is called social distancing. The reason for social distancing is to keep germs away from living creatures.

This meant that Limoncello should not gather with her friends at school or for fun after school. This was very hard to do. When Limoncello had to go out where other creatures might be she made sure to cover her face. This would help to keep germs away too.

4. Talk to a Doctor if you have a fever, cough, or trouble breathing.

5. Exercise and stay fit.

Limoncello would practice Yoga everyday. Yoga was very hard for plump little ducks yet Limoncello persisted.

Limoncello also would dance, hike, and swim in her pond. This was not hard at all for her to do every day. In fact, it was quite fun! Especially the dancing!

6. Nourish your body.

Limoncello would nourish her whole body. This
included her stomach, mind, heart, and soul.

Limoncello would eat healthy and fresh meals to nourish her stomach. She would read books and play guitar and sing songs to nourish her mind, heart, and soul.

7. Stay connected to your family, friends, and teachers.

Limoncello had to think hard about how to connect with others. How do you stay connected to others when staying away from others was also really important? Then Limoncello knew what to do! She would text her friends and take Zoom classes to help stay connected to others.

Limoncello was a thoughtful, smart, and kind duck and happy to do her part. She created a plan of action so she and her friends and family would not forget to do any of the seven things the Doctors talked about.

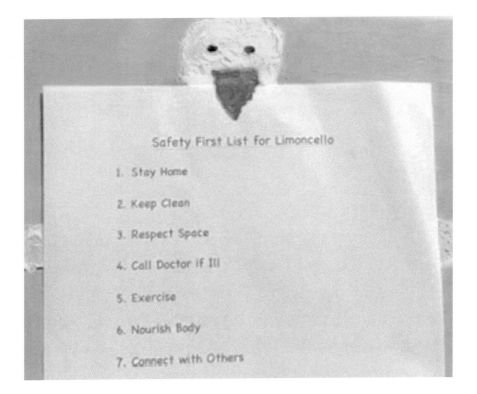

Safety First List for Limoncello

1. Stay Home

2. Keep Clean

3. Respect Space

4. Call Doctor if Ill

5. Exercise

6. Nourish Body

7. Connect with Others

Limoncello and her family and friends paid attention to the Doctors and followed their plan.   The illness finally went away. Limoncello was safe!

Limoncello was very proud of her friends and family
for all they did to stay safe and healthy during
The Great Illness.

Limoncello was amazed that the pond was bluer, the sky and stars a little more brilliant, and the lazy little meadow with the welcoming wildflowers clearer and brighter after the illness had passed through.

Limoncello was always a very happy little duck.
After The Great Illness she became a very grateful
little duck too.

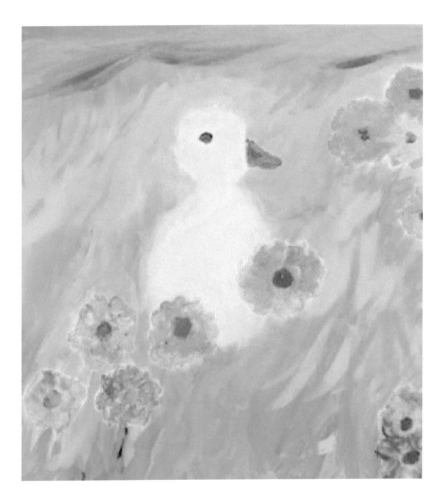

Made in the USA
Monee, IL
13 February 2021

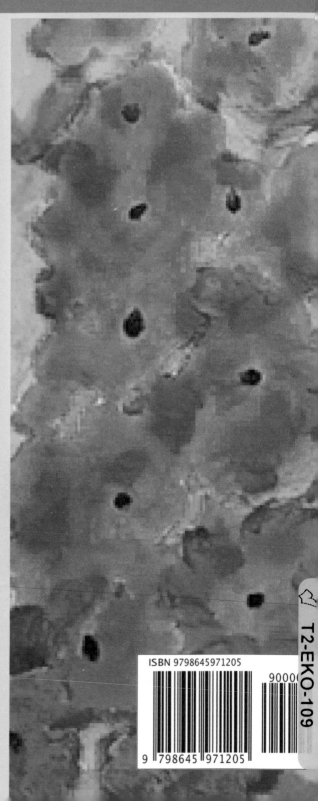

ISBN 9798645971205

9 798645 971205

90000

T2-EKO-109

My Colors, My World
Mis colores, mi mundo

Christina Gonzalez